£23.48

helping learners to
PRACTISE
the **official** guide

London: TSO

Written and compiled by Driving Standards Agency (DSA) Publications.

Published with the permission of the Driving Standards Agency on behalf of the Controller of Her Majesty's Stationery Office.

© Crown copyright 2004.

All rights reserved. Applications for reproduction should be made in writing to Commercial Department, Driving Standards Agency, Stanley House, 56 Talbot Street, Nottingham, NG1 5GU.

This title was formerly known as The Official Guide to Accompanying Learner Drivers

First published 2000
Second edition 2004

ISBN 0 11 2611 0

A CIP catalogue record for this book is available from the British Library.

Other titles in the Driving series

The Official Theory Test for Car Drivers
The Official Theory Test for Motorcyclists
The Official Theory Test for Drivers of Large Vehicles
Driving - the essential skills
The Official Guide to Learning to Drive
Motorcycle Riding – the essential skills
Official Motorcycling – CBT and practical test
Driving Buses and Coaches – the official DSA syllabus
Driving Goods Vehicles – the official DSA syllabus
The Official Guide to Tractor and Specialist Vehicle Driving Tests
The Official Theory Test CD-Rom – for car drivers
The Official Theory Test CD-Rom – for motorcyclists
The Official Guide to Hazard Perception DVD
Roadsense – the official guide to hazard perception VHS
The Official Guide to Learning to Drive DVD

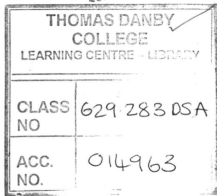

Acknowledgements

The Driving Standards Agency would like to thank their staff and the following organisations for their contribution to the production of this publication:

Department for Transport

Driver and Vehicle Testing Agency

Bedfordshire Constabulary

Every effort has been made to ensure that the information contained in this publication is accurate at the time of going to press. The Stationery Office cannot be held responsible for any inaccuracies. Information in this book is for guidance only.

All metric and imperial conversions in this book are approximate.

Theory and practical tests

(Bookings and enquiries)

DSA **0870 01 01 372**
Fax **0870 01 04 372**
Minicom **0870 01 06 372**
Welsh speakers **0870 01 00 372**

DVTA (Northern Ireland)
Theory test **0845 600 6700**
Practical test **0870 247 2472**

Driving Standards Agency

(Headquarters)

Stanley House, 56 Talbot Street,
Nottingham NG1 5GU

Tel **0115 901 2500**
Fax **0115 901 2510**

Driver and Vehicle Testing Agency

(Headquarters)

Balmoral Road, Belfast BT12 6QL

Tel **02890 681831**
Fax **02890 665520**

Driver and Vehicle Licensing Agency

(GB Licence Enquiries)

Tel **0870 240 0009**
Fax **01792 783071**
Minicom **01792 782787**

Driver and Vehicle Licensing

(Northern Ireland)

Tel **02870 341469**
24 hour tel **0345 111 222**
Minicom **02870 341 380**

Mobility Advice and Vehicle Information Service

'O' Wing, MacAdam Avenue,
Old Wokingham Road, Crowthorne
Berkshire RG45 6XD

Tel **01344 661000**
Fax **01344 661066**

The Driving Standards Agency (DSA) is an executive agency of the Department for Transport. You'll see its logo at test centres.

DSA aims to promote road safety through the advancement of driving standards, by

- establishing and developing high standards and best practice in driving and riding on the road; before people start to drive, as they learn, and after they pass their test
- ensuring high standards of instruction for different types of driver and rider
- conducting the statutory theory and practical tests efficiently, fairly and consistently across the country
- providing a centre of excellence for driver training and driving standards
- developing a range of publications and other publicity material designed to promote safe driving for life.

www.dsa.gov.uk

The Driver and Vehicle Testing Agency (DVTA) is an executive agency within the Department of the Environment for Northern Ireland.

Its primary aim is to promote and improve road safety through the advancement of driving standards and implementation of the Government's policies for improving the mechanical standards of vehicles.

www.doeni.gov.uk/dvta

CONTENTS

Section one
ACCOMPANYING A LEARNER DRIVER

Section two
KEY SKILLS

Section two continued...

Section three
OTHER INFORMATION

ANNEX

section **one**
ACCOMPANYING
A LEARNER DRIVER

This section covers
- about this book
- structured learning
- getting started
- attitude
- planning

A message from the Chief Driving Examiner

First the bad news

On average, ten people die every day on the UK's roads and hundreds more are seriously injured.

Newly qualified drivers account for far more than their fair share of these accidents. Check the insurance premiums of a new driver against those of an experienced driver. That will give an idea of how big a risk new drivers are known to be.

Now for the good news

Statistics show that the risk to newly qualified drivers decreases with miles driven and experience gained. If that experience is gained before the driving test is passed then the likelihood of an accident in those first few critical months can be reduced.

The key to it all is practice. Driving a motor car is a complex business that takes much longer to master than most people appreciate. Rushing to take the driving test before enough experience has been gained is a mistake. About half the people who present themselves for their practical driving test haven't mastered basic driving skills.

However, those who have had plenty of practice on a variety of roads, and at different times of the day and night, are more likely to pass their driving test at the first attempt and go on to have a reduced risk of accident in their early years of driving unaccompanied.

Driving is a complex and exciting activity but one not to be taken lightly. To almost ten people every day in the UK it is also a fatal activity. Getting enough practice of the right type before passing the driving test is a big step towards achieving 'Safe driving for life'.

Robin Cummins

Robin Cummins
The Chief Driving Examiner
Driving Standards Agency

About this book

This book is aimed at those experienced drivers who want to help a learner driver gain driving experience through practice.

Remember, not everyone can legally accompany a learner driver. Check that you can on p14.

It's not a driving instruction manual but a guide to help with questions such as 'When?', 'Where?' and 'How much?' while offering guidance to help steer around some of the pitfalls and problems that may arise.

Being a passenger in your own car with a learner driving can be an unsettling experience. Keeping in mind your reason for being there should help; and take comfort from the fact that accidents while learning are very rare indeed.

Books to help

It is strongly recommended that you have a current copy of *The Highway Code* handy for reference. You can buy one from any good bookshop and many other outlets.

The DSA official series of products provide a good source of knowledge of driving skills and safe practices.

The Official Guide to Learning to Drive (book and interactive DVD), The Official Theory Test for Car Drivers (book and CD-Rom), Driving - the essential skills and *Know Your Traffic Signs* are also available.

These, and other official training materials, are available by mail order from **0870 241 4523**. They are also available from all good bookshops and other outlets.

Or buy online at **www.dsa.gov.uk**

Accompanying a learner

To learn how to drive, the Driving Standards Agency (DSA) recommends a structured learning programme, with a combination of formal tuition and private practice.

Formal driving tuition can **only** be given by either a trainee or a qualified Approved Driving Instructor (ADI) (see p53) who can also help structure the private practice. Look on the process of making your relative or friend a safe driver as a team effort involving you, your learner and their ADI.

If you feel unsure about anything or want a bit of advice, you can talk to the ADI about the areas which concern you. You may want to accompany your learner on their next lesson to see how the ADI copes with situations you find difficult. Make sure your learner is happy for you to sit in on their lesson and arrange a suitable time with the ADI.

Sometimes you may think the ADI is teaching a driving technique which seems wrong to you. Remember, as cars become more sophisticated, so recommended techniques change to take advantage of new technology.

Remember, working together is the best way of ensuring everyone's aim of safe driving for life.

The ADI is probably using the most up-to-date methods which may be different to the way you were taught. Don't confuse your learner by expecting them to do things 'your way'. One part of your role is to enable your learner to practise the techniques taught by their ADI.

Structured learning

The Driver's Record

The *Driver's Record* is a pocket-sized leaflet that your learner may have received with their provisional licence or the ADI may have issued one to your learner.

The *Driver's Record* provides a structured learning programme and it can be very helpful for

- learners to keep track of their progress
- letting your learner know the topics to practise
- letting the ADI know how you, and your learner, have got on.

The *Driver's Record* contains a list of all the 24 Key Skills in which your learner needs to reach the required standard to pass the practical driving test and become a safe driver. As your learner progresses the ADI will record their performance using the various levels shown on the Record.

See the page opposite to find out more about the five levels.

The Driver's Record will help to remind you what you're trying to achieve, how to get there and how far you've got

10

What are the five levels?

Each of the 24 Key Skills in the *Driver's Record*, is broken down into five levels which represent each stage of learning.

1 the skill is introduced

2 it can be carried out under full instruction

3 it can be carried out correctly when prompted

4 it seldom needs to be prompted

5 you can carry it out consistently without any prompting

Levels one to four should be initialled and dated by your ADI, and full details added when **Level 5** is being consistently reached.

From this, you can see at a glance which topics need improvement.

The 24 Key Skills are covered in detail by section two (p22-51).

Where can I get hold of a Driver's Record?

If you haven't got one, ask your instructor, get one from your local driving test centre or download one from **www.dsa.gov.uk**

The annex on p56 contains part of the *Driver's Record* which you can use to record any sessions that you have had without your instructor (known as private practice).

You will need to record details such as the type of roads used and the weather conditions so that your ADI is up to date with the type of experience your learner is receiving.

If your learner picks up good habits now they'll be safer once they are on the road on their own

Getting started

Beginning

For a new driver there's an awful lot to learn. The list includes

- a good knowledge of driving theory
- learning how to operate a complicated set of controls (which looks so easy)
- operating the controls while putting the theory into practice
- developing good judgement
- anticipation and awareness.

As well as developing these skills they need to learn to cope with

- other road users
- the weather
- road conditions
- navigation.

> **Remember,** new drivers cannot begin driving until they have received their licence from the Driver and Vehicle Licensing Agency (DVLA) and it has come into effect.

Even after basic control skills have developed, being able to cope with constantly changing demands and unexpected events – often in a fraction of a second – are skills which come with experience.

The whole business is complicated, challenging and, for some, extremely difficult. To expect that all this can be learned in a few short lessons is a mistake.

A learner driver needs to gain enough skill and experience to enable them to drive alone safely once they have passed their driving test. As more miles are driven and more experience is gained, the novice driver will gradually progress towards becoming an experienced driver.

However, driving is a subject where there are always new lessons to be learned and it is a foolish and dangerous driver who thinks they know it all.

So how does a learner begin the process of going from novice to competent safe driver? The answer lies in two key areas

Training – to learn new skills

Practice – to gain experience.

Training

Most people learn to drive with an ADI. Driving instructors are professionals who are trained to teach driving skills in a structured manner to suit differing abilities.

Remember, some insurance companies don't insure people under 25 years of age, while others may offer reduced premiums for new drivers who complete the Pass Plus scheme (see p55).

Don't risk driving uninsured!

Many pupils only have one or two hours of professional driving instruction each week and their experience is often limited to driving at the same time of day and over the same types of roads.

Four levels of learning to drive

Danger of overconfidence

1 **Unconscious incompetence**
We don't know that we don't know

Ignorance

2 **Conscious incompetence**
We know that we don't know

Take driving lessons

3 **Conscious competence**
We do it but we have to concentrate really hard

Practice - The hard part is going from 3 to 4 without getting dejected

4 **Unconscious competence**
We do it so naturally we can think about other things at the same time

Awareness and anticipation

If you want to take part in the Pass Plus scheme please call 0115 901 2633 or visit our website at www.passplus.org.uk

PASS PLUS

Where you fit in

As an accompanying driver you will be helping your learner have more practice and gain wider experience of the varied driving conditions they are likely to meet once they have passed their driving test.

However, there are a few things to consider before you start (see below).

Once you are ready to take on this responsibility you need to think about developing the skills of your learner - know their limits and don't attempt any driving which will be beyond their ability.

You're helping a new driver to gain skills which will help to keep them safe for many years to come.

That's not to say it will be an easy task and there may be times when you need to remind yourself why you're there.

Don't forget that only an ADI can charge for driving lessons. Even accepting money for fuel is an offence unless you're an ADI. Don't be caught out.

> **Remember**, learners who combine extra practice with professional lessons not only perform better on their driving test but go on to have a reduced accident rate in the early years of driving unaccompanied.

Can you do it legally?

Before you agree to accompany a learner driver there are a few things you need to check:

1 have you held a full EC/EEA driving licence for at least three years for the category of vehicle being driven?

2 are you at least 21 years of age?

3 is the car you intend to use insured for use by the learner?

4 is the car fitted with L-plates (D-plates in Wales) to both the front and rear of the car?

5 is the car you intend to use in a safe roadworthy condition?

The answer must be YES to all questions before you can act as an accompanying driver to a learner.

What can you expect?

To start with, don't expect this to be easy. Learning to drive takes a lot longer than most people realise. You need to set aside plenty of your time for practice sessions so there are no excuses.

If you set dates and times when you're expecting to go out with your learner, you're more likely to be in a calm frame of mind than if you've had to stop what you were doing and grudgingly give your time.

Be guided by the ADI, but once the basic skills have been learned it's a good idea to let your learner do a lot of the everyday driving, such as to the shops or to school or college.

Some learners struggle with the clutch, others with the gears. The key is to be patient

If your driver struggles with something you think is easy, don't worry. Everyone learns at different rates and in different ways and it may be necessary to go over the same ground many times.

Memory often plays tricks and you may have forgotten how you struggled with some aspects of learning to drive.

> **Remember,** young drivers are about twice as likely to have an accident negotiating a bend than older drivers.

What are you expecting to achieve? -

The goals you should be aiming for are a new driver who

- has practised their new skills until they are both confident and competent
- has a sound basis on which to build their driving career
- has gained enough experience to be able to think for themselves and cope safely with any driving situation
- will be confident about their ability to pass the driving test
- understands their responsibility as a driver.

The practice vehicle

Is your car suitable for your learner to drive?- A learner may learn in any make or model of car but a large, powerful car may be more difficult to control than a smaller model.

Small cars are not necessarily any easier to drive but their size can make judging the car's position easier, especially during manoeuvres.

It might be helpful to find a driving school that uses a similar car to your own. If this isn't possible, make allowances for your learner if they struggle to adapt to your car after lessons in the school car.

Make sure the L-plates are secure, you don't want them to fly off once you try higher speed roads

Remember, fit an extra rear view mirror. Knowing what's going on behind is important for safety and peace of mind.

L-plates - Avoid fixing L (D) plates to the windscreen or rear window since they restrict the view. Don't forget to cover or remove the L (D) plates when the car is being used by a full licence holder.

Attitude

Bad habits

It's too easy for bad habits to creep unnoticed into anyone's driving. Before you act as an accompanying driver it's worth looking at your own driving. You'll have little credibility if you expect your learner to drive one way while you practise another – and don't expect your learner not to notice. Why not have a lesson or two with the ADI yourself? This will allow an expert to check your driving and help you to improve your skills.

Drinking and driving, speed limits, use of signals, seat belts and attitude to other road users are all aspects of driving where standards slip. Setting a good example when you drive will have positive benefits for both you and your learner.

Patience

Frustration can soon set in when your learner struggles with something you think should be easy, or can't do something that they could do the last time you went out. If something is proving difficult, don't keep on until tempers fray. Leave it and come back to it another time. Learning to drive should be an enjoyable experience, not an ordeal.

Other road users may be inconsiderate and show little regard for the fact that your driver is a learner. Don't allow this to wind you up since it will also affect your learner. Knocking a learner driver's confidence can ruin their driving career before it has even started.

Technique

Before accompanying your learner you should give some thought to how you are going to

- give directions
- cope with dangerous situations.

> **Remember,** learning to drive takes a lot longer than most people think.
>
> **Be patient with your learner.**

Your learner will need clear directions given calmly and in plenty of time. You will need to look and think that bit further ahead than normal. If your learner has difficulty telling their right from their left you'll need to overcome this problem. Your ADI should be able to give you some advice on these matters, as well as tips on giving directions at any complex junctions in your area.

Safety is your first priority and, where possible, you should act early and prevent hazards from developing into dangerous situations. If a dangerous situation does develop, you may need to

- speak firmly and clearly without shouting
- reach across and take control of the steering
- use the handbrake
- use dual controls if fitted.

Avoiding conflicts

Accompanying a novice driver can be frustrating, unnerving and a lot harder than you think. Here are a few points worth remembering to help you keep on top of it.

- Talking to the ADI will help you plan practice sessions which avoid areas that are too difficult for your learner's present level of ability

- Learn from mistakes and don't dwell on them. Encouragement and tolerance will help skills and confidence develop

- Nothing is achieved if you allow yourself to become angry with your learner. If it's all going wrong have a break for five minutes or stop the session altogether if things are too bad

- If something happens which scares either of you, pull over and give yourselves time to calm down. Discuss what went wrong and why. Were you expecting too much from your learner?

- If another road user fails to show your learner due consideration, don't allow it to upset you. Set a good example, keep calm and turn the experience into a lesson in anticipation

Remember, keep reminding yourself that you're making a big difference to your learner's long-term driving safety. Learners rarely have crashes while practising.

- Prevent your learner from getting into difficulties by looking well ahead so you can anticipating problems. Don't expect them to have the same degree of awareness and judgement as you

- Your learner is going to drive in the way their instructor has taught. If any techniques differ from the way you drive don't argue over who's right or insist they do it your way. Make a note and discuss it with the ADI.

Planning

When to start

DSA recommends that new drivers reach a level of proficiency with an ADI before starting to practise with an accompanying driver. Ask the ADI to tell you when your learner is ready to start practising. Starting too soon may be unnerving for both of you and could lead to anything from a loss of confidence through to a serious loss of control.

> **Remember,** a learner driver may find driving very tiring. Many crashes involving young drivers result from lack of experience.

Use the *Driver's Record* to see the progress being made and the topics needing practice. To start with, this will be mostly control skills but will gradually move on to include the whole syllabus.

Early days

Before you begin your first practice sessions, you need to give some thought to where and when. Driving in heavy traffic at rush hour isn't going to be good for either of you.

Where - Pick a quiet area where

- there won't be much traffic to deal with
- you won't cause a nuisance to other road users or local residents.

It's also a good idea to find somewhere fairly level because of the added difficulties a hill can create at this stage.

Your learner will probably drive quite slowly and, despite your efforts to find somewhere quiet, you may find a queue of traffic building up behind. If this happens, be prepared to ask your learner to pull over somewhere safe and let it pass.

When - Plan the first few practice sessions to avoid busy times of the day. These include

- rush hours
- school start and finish times
- during local events.

Your learner can only practise when you make the time available. Work and other commitments may make demands on you and the only time you have could be evenings and weekends.

In the winter months, evening practice will be in the dark – but don't let this be an excuse not to practise. As long as the weather conditions aren't dangerous, practising in the dark shouldn't be a problem.

Planning your sessions

Many learners take their driving lessons at the same time of day and drive repeatedly over the same types of roads.

> **Remember,** could your learner cope with any situation that might arise? They will have to when they pass their test.

While this may provide a level of familiarity with these roads, it does little to provide a broad experience of the wide variety of driving conditions your learner will meet when they have passed their test.

Good practice sessions should build both experience and confidence. This can be achieved by planning each session around your learner's requirements and their driving limitations. Refer to their *Driver's Record* to see which topics need practising.

As part of your planning you will need to think about routes, time of day, road types, manoeuvring and weather conditions. These are now looked at in turn:

Routes - Thinking through where you are going to take your learner will enable you to

- avoid areas which may have features such as a steep hill or a difficult junction which they are not yet ready to encounter
- practise certain aspects such as left turns, traffic lights, one way streets, etc.

You don't want to find you have put your learner into a situation which they can't cope with and could have been avoided if you had planned ahead.

Time of day - Local knowledge will enable you to know which roads are busiest and when. This will enable you to avoid the worst areas in the early days, and practise in busy traffic when your learner is ready.

Daylight, dusk and darkness are all driving conditions which need different skills and need to be practised. If your learner has great difficulty seeing at night, get their night vision tested by an optician. Your learner should be able to think independently and use the car's lights when necessary.

Road types - While a learner cannot use a motorway, they can drive on all other types of road. For example, driving on a dual carriageway calls for skills and techniques that will need to be learned and practised.

If a *Driver's Record* is being used it will indicate the types of road where practice is needed.

Manoeuvring - The driving test requires manoeuvres to be demonstrated which reflect real driving situations. These include stopping in an emergency, turning the car around in the road, reversing into a side road and parking using reverse gear, both on the road and into car park bays.

The ADI will teach the techniques and, if a *Driver's Record* is being used, will record which have been taught and which need practice.

Weather conditions - Many learners begin learning in the spring months and pass the driving test before winter arrives.

> **Remember,** don't underestimate the weather. Extreme weather can make driving unsafe and it's recommended that you avoid practising in these conditions in the early days.
>
> **If in doubt - don't venture out**

These learners may have had little or no experience of driving in

- rain and slippery conditions
- mist and fog
- windy conditions

These are everyday conditions that most motorists encounter in their first year of driving. When the ADI indicates your learner is ready to cope with them, be prepared to go out in these conditions as they occur.

section two
KEY SKILLS

This section covers

- legal responsibilities
- safety checks
- controls and instruments
- cockpit checks

- moving away & stopping
- mirrors - vision and use
- safe positioning
- signals
- anticipation and planning
- use of speed
- other traffic
- junctions
- roundabouts
- pedestrian crossings
- dual carriageways
- turning the vehicle around
- reversing
- parking
- emergency stop
- darkness
- weather conditions
- environmental issues
- passengers and loads
- security

Legal responsibilities

At **Level 5** your learner should have a full understanding of their legal responsibilities as a driver.

> **Remember,** that ignorance is no excuse in the eyes of the law. Make sure you are both up to date.

They will need to know about their legal responsibilities including

- driving licences and accompanying learner drivers
- road tax (SORN), insurance and MOT
- health and eyesight
- New Drivers Act
- tiredness and rest periods
- traffic rules and regulations
- alcohol and drugs
- mobile phones
- vehicle condition
- dealing with accidents.

How you can help

Ask questions so that your learner has to think about their responsibilities. If you are both unclear about an issue then work together to find out the facts. For example, if you didn't know about the New Drivers Act, you could ask your ADI to explain it to you both.

What to expect

Many new drivers will have an understanding of the issues that directly affect them such as applying for a driving licence. They may not know about recent changes in the law or matters that you routinely deal with such as taxing your car.

Keep a current copy of The Highway Code in your car so that you can keep up to date

If you involve your learner they may not only learn the processes but they may also appreciate the costs associated with owning and running a motor car.

To keep up to date with changes in the law, own and refer to the latest edition of *The Highway Code.*

Cockpit checks

Your learner will have reached **Level 5** for this topic when they independently

- make a point of checking their door is closed properly
- check and, if necessary, adjust their driving position. This includes adjusting the seat, steering wheel, head restraints
- correctly fasten their seat belt
- check and adjust the mirrors
- check the handbrake is on and the gear lever is in neutral.

How you can help

Watch to see that they complete their checks before starting the engine. Look to see that each item is checked and not just mentioned.

What to expect

It is not uncommon for learners to find that once they are on the road, one or more mirrors require some further adjustment or the seat needs re-positioning.

Do not let them try to make adjustments while on the move, but find a safe place for them to pull over and stop before making any further adjustments.

Mirrors need to be adjusted so that they can be used with the least possible head movement

Safety checks

As a part of their driving test your learner will be asked to show and explain basic safety checks necessary to keep their car safe on the road.

These questions are published on the DSA web site www.dsa.gov.uk

Your ADI will cover the driving test requirements but learning how to carry out routine safety checks is not something to learn for the test and then forget. Aspects, such as the condition of the tyres, are the driver's responsibility and, if the tyres are illegal, the driver could be fined or have penalty points added to their driving licence.

How you can help

Before each practice drive watch while your learner carries out safety checks on your vehicle.

Developing a habit of regular checks can also help identify faults at an early stage and this may prevent the vehicle breaking down during a journey. Allowing your learner to clean the windscreen, windows, mirrors and lights will help you and help them to remember these aspects.

How can I remember the safety checks?

Just remember POWER if you have problems with your safety checks.

P petrol

O oil (engine, brake fluid)

W water (engine coolant, windscreen washers)

E electrics (lights, indicators)

R rubber and brakes.

What to expect

Many new drivers do not have an interest in the workings of the car but they do need to understand

- daily and weekly vehicle checks
- service intervals
- MOT requirements.

The importance of having your vehicle regularly serviced should be stressed and you could show how you keep a record of your car's service intervals.

Controls and instruments

Reading and understanding instruments such as the speedometer, fuel and temperature gauge are essential.

By the time your learner is ready for their test they should also understand the warning lamps and, importantly, know what action to take if one comes on while they are driving.

In the early days of learning to drive, controlling the steering, gears and foot controls will take all your learner's concentration.

Remember, your learner should be able to operate all the controls without having to look down to find them.

As their skill develops it's important for them to become competent with ancillary controls such as demister, wipers, heaters, etc.

How you can help

Allow your learner to familiarise themselves with the layout of the controls and instruments and explain any special features that may be fitted to your car.

The controls may be laid out differently in the ADI's car and this could lead to some confusion, for example, windscreen wiper controls on the left of the steering column or on the right.

What to expect

When you're in situations that call for the use of certain controls, such as the front or rear screen demister, your learner may be concentrating really hard on their driving and fail to realise the need to use them.

Don't allow the situation to become dangerous, but do encourage your learner to recognise for themselves when these controls should be used.

If your learner fumbles while trying to find and operate the control they want, pull up somewhere safe and run through the control layout again.

Moving away and stopping

To move away safely your learner will need skill in use of the controls as well as

- sound judgement
- awareness of other road users.

Choosing a safe place to stop and stopping safely is both a requirement of the driving test and something that every driver needs to do.

How you can help

To begin with, it's best to practise moving off on a level surface, progressing to sloping surfaces as skill develops.

While your learner is having to concentrate really hard on using the controls, they may forget to watch for other road users. Stay alert and don't let them move off into danger.

Practise moving off

- on the level
- uphill
- downhill
- from behind a parked vehicle.

Asking your learner to pick somewhere safe to stop will allow them to think for themselves. They need to look for somewhere safe to stop and then use their mirrors and signals correctly while bringing the car to rest at their chosen place.

What to expect

Every time your learner moves off, unless you are in a car with automatic transmission, expect them to go through a lengthy process of finding the biting point and balancing the accelerator and clutch against the handbrake. This will make moving off a slow process and this in turn makes dealing with road junctions more difficult.

Remember, traffic lights are one place where tension can build. When the red light changes it's not uncommon for novices to stall in their rush to move off promptly. This can lead to panic, especially if there's a queue of traffic behind. Stay calm and don't react to another driver sounding their horn – they may not be able to see the L-plates if they're not immediately behind.

At busy junctions frustration may set in as

- traffic builds up behind
- your learner can't pull out into a space which you would find safe as a driver.

If you find your learner has difficulty with busy junctions avoid them until the necessary control skills have developed.

When stopping, watch that they don't try to stop suddenly without allowing time for using the mirror and signalling if necessary. Use the extra rear view mirror to check the traffic behind you.

Safe positioning

With experience, judging the car's position becomes second nature, but learning to position accurately is a surprisingly difficult skill to learn.

Some learners look just in front of the car rather than well ahead. This makes it more difficult to judge the car's width and position on the road. As well as the control skills, your learner will need to know

- where to position the car for any particular driving situation
- the meaning of signs and road markings.

How you can help

The skill of being able to judge the car's position on the road from the passenger seat will develop with practice. You may need to reach across and steer into the correct position. Try to remain calm and don't allow the wrong road position to go uncorrected for any length of time.

In the early days, avoid taking your learner into places where you know accurate judgement is called for, such as a narrow street or roads with width restrictions.

What to expect

Before your learner's judgement has developed you can expect to see

- driving too close to the edge of the road, parked cars, other obstructions, the centre of the road
- poor positioning around bends and junctions
- poor lane discipline.

Some of these mistakes can be quite scary for you in the passenger seat and it's quite likely that your learner will be unaware of both their error and the way their positioning is making you feel.

Remember, don't allow your learner to hit the kerb while driving normally. The impact may wrench the steering wheel from their grasp causing serious loss of control. Alternatively it may damage or burst the tyre.

If it's going wrong, pull over and talk about any specific problems. Your learner may not think there is anything wrong and you may need to demonstrate their mistake in order for them to see it themselves. If you have a disagreement over where you should position the car, then refer it to the ADI.

Mirrors - vision and use

The ADI will teach the use of mirrors early on in the training process. As part of the cockpit checks the mirrors should have been checked and adjusted so that minimal head movement should be required to use them.

If your learner is having to make exaggerated head movements to use the mirrors, it probably needs re-adjusting. They will need to pull up in a safe place before doing so.

Correctly adjusted mirrors will give a good view both behind and to the sides of the car. It's important that your learner uses the mirrors when necessary and is aware of the areas not covered by the mirrors (and that they know how and when to check them).

How you can help

When accompanying your learner look to see if they are checking their mirror correctly. If a mirror check is missed you should always draw their attention to it but avoid prompting

them too early or they may become reliant on your prompt and not think for themselves. Don't let them change direction without first having checked that it is safe to do so.

> **Remember,** when turning right in busy traffic there will be occasions when a blind area check to the right needs to be made in case a vehicle is attempting to overtake. There may be so much else going on that this check is missed and you may need to look for them.

To check if your learner is using their mirrors, fit another small interior mirror on the left of the windscreen, angled so that you can see your learner without having to look directly at them.

What to expect

When watching your learner's use of their mirrors check

- how well they time their mirror checks
- that they act correctly on what can be seen.

You may find yourself having to look and plan further ahead than normal so that you can identify hazards early enough to be then watching to see how your learner deals with them. This can have an extra benefit in that it improves your own hazard awareness.

Signals

Drivers need to know how and when to give signals and the meaning of signals given by others. Whether signals are given by arm, indicators, or any other type of signalling device, they must be given clearly and in good time. In cases where a signal is being given by another road user your learner must be able to identify their signal and act correctly.

How you can help

Watch your learner's use of signals and make sure they use only signals shown in *The Highway Code*. Try and cover routes that will expose your learner to the need to think about the timing of a signal or whether a signal is appropriate.

Examples could be

- when passing a parked car with a road junction on the right
- turning right or left when there is another junction just before your turn.

If you are in any doubt about the correct procedure for a local junction or road layout ask the ADI for advice.

What to expect

In the early days learners will be thinking about their use of the car controls and may forget to signal. This may be dangerous, for example, when pulling up while being followed by another vehicle. Remain alert and give help in good time if safety is threatened.

There may be occasions where another road user gives a signal that your learner hasn't met before, for example, reversing lights on a car that is trying to reverse park into a space on the side of the road.

Learners tend to shy away from using the horn. However, it is a valuable aid to road safety when used correctly and you should encourage its use when appropriate.

Most indicators will automatically cancel after a manoeuvre but they may not. Don't let an uncancelled signal continue for any length of time - it could mislead another road user and lead to danger.

Anticipation and Planning

Before your learner can react to a risk they must perceive that a risk exists. That perception is governed by

- training (in this situation do this)
- experience (I've met this before and need to do this)
- planning (what should I do now to prevent risk in the situation I can see?)
- anticipation (what if?)

One of the main problems for inexperienced drivers is that they don't recognise the hazard until it is too late to avoid the danger. That is why practice is so important.

> **Remember,** new drivers often don't look very far ahead. They can be too slow to identify potential danger and don't realise how soon they need to react.
>
> **Step in to help before danger develops**

How you can help

During practice your learner will meet situations that they have never met before.

While you're sat next to them, your experience in both seeing and reacting to any risk should keep them safe and where possible you can pass on the benefit of your experience.

Your learner will never experience every type of hazard but what you can aim for is to instil a heightened awareness of hazards and a knowledge of how to cope with them.

What to expect

Your learner may feel they have everything under control but you may not feel that way. If the way your learner is dealing with hazards makes you feel uncomfortable, something is wrong with their driving.

When a mistake has been made you'll need to tell him or her that their response to a situation or hazard was potentially dangerous. Keep calm and don't raise your voice.

Learners can be defensive about their driving ability and you should take account of their feelings. However, you do need to make sure they understand the consequences of their actions.

Use of speed

Driving too fast is one of the main causes of road accidents on all types of roads. Driving too slowly is a different mistake and one that creates its own set of hazards.

They need to be aware of changes in the speed limit

So how fast should your learner be driving? What is a suitable speed? The answer is dependent on a number of variables and getting it right takes practice.

Your learner must never drive beyond their ability or the speed limit, but they will need to reach a level where they can drive on all roads without hindering the flow of traffic.

How you can help

The more practice your learner can have of various driving situations the better they'll become at assessing the correct speed to suit different conditions.

If you have a timid driver remember that timid people take a long time to feel confident with making progress.

If you think your learner is not improving very quickly, don't be negative or critical - a timid driver needs encouragement not criticism. Learning to drive is a lengthy process and you just need to allow more time and more practice.

Don't ignore rural roads where wide variations in speed can be experienced and they will have to

- plan ahead
- continually adjust their speed.

What to expect

You can expect your learner to start by driving slowly in all situations. In particular, expect very slow acceleration up through the gears, which can make emerging at junctions difficult and for you, frustrating.

In the early days don't let your learner drive the car if you're in a hurry to get somewhere since this may make you feel impatient.

If you're critical and negative, what sort of message do you think this gives your learner about correct driver behaviour towards other road users?

> **Remember,** make sure your learner obeys speed limits and understands that they are not targets, they're the maximum speed legally permitted.
>
> **That doesn't mean it's always safe to drive up to the speed limit.**

You need to be patient, tolerant and understanding.

As experience and confidence develop, speeds will increase and skills in hazard awareness and planning ahead will need to develop. However, overconfidence and an irresponsible attitude towards risk need to be guarded against.

The ADI will teach your learner how to keep a safe distance from the vehicle in front, but they must then put this theory into practice when they drive.

It's vital that your learner understands that they are responsible for the consequences of their driving behaviour

Applying the two-second rule (see *Driving - the essential skills*) is not a complicated procedure, but you may find your learner simply forgets to apply it. This can lead to driving too close to the vehicle in front and being unaware of the risk.

Sitting next to anyone who is driving too close to the vehicle in front can be unsettling and it's important that you make your learner aware of their mistake straight away.

Other traffic

Your learner needs to gain experience of dealing with traffic while having the safety net of an experienced driver sitting by their side. They are never going to encounter every possible situation but should be able to safely deal with

- meeting oncoming traffic
- turning across the path of other vehicles
- overtaking
- parked vehicles or other obstructions.

How you can help

These traffic situations call for judgement and often there is little or no room for error.

> **Remember,** you are responsible for ensuring your learner does not create a dangerous situation through their inexperience or lack of judgement.

Don't allow your learner to overestimate their own ability or their car's performance. If they make a mistake you're there to prevent it developing into something more serious.

You can help by avoiding busy main roads until confidence has developed. Find places to practise that will include

- narrow roads
  - parked cars and other obstructions
    - roads with right-turn lane markings
    - traffic lights
    - box junctions.

Don't just practise dealing with obstructions on your side of the road. Find places where your learner has to anticipate the actions of an approaching driver who might not give way.

For hazards that you don't encounter you can talk to your learner about possible situations. Thinking about potential danger is a big part of developing hazard awareness.

*When meeting oncoming traffic your learner needs to judge the available space and,
if necessary, give way*

What to expect

Learners will usually err on the side of caution.
If the road is busy this might mean waiting for
some time. Don't allow yourself to become
frustrated because your learner won't take
opportunities that seem reasonable to you.
As their confidence builds, so will their ability.

When waiting to turn right you may find
oncoming drivers give way and invite your
learner to complete turning. Before accepting
this offer your learner must check for
other road users, especially motorcyclists
and cyclists.

There are many mistakes that may be made
when overtaking, some more hazardous than
others. Watch for your learner making errors
born of inexperience and lack of judgement.
These can include

- overtaking too slowly
- overtaking when the vehicle in front is
  driving at close to the speed limit
- not allowing enough room
- cutting in too soon after overtaking.

If your car is different to the ADI's your learner
may take time to get used to judging its width.

Junctions

Practising dealing with junctions doesn't just mean turning right and left, but driving straight ahead as well. Junctions come in all shapes and sizes including those with

- no road markings
- road markings
- road markings and warning signs
- traffic lights.

Your learner will have to learn where and when they should be looking, and what it is they are looking for. Interpreting what they see and planning how to deal with the possible outcomes is a skill which develops with experience.

It's likely that your learner will have studied for their theory test and learnt the meanings of all the road signs and markings in *The Highway Code*. Putting the theory into practice might not be so easy. The learner driver has to first see the sign or markings and realise it affects them before acting on the information given.

Remember, don't let your learner's apparent confidence fool you – their hazard perception skills will not be well developed, even though they think they are observing well and feel they have everything under control.

It's important to explain the importance of assessing whether another road user has seen you when dealing with junctions - it may take a while for them develop this ability

Correctly timed signals help other road users know your learner's intentions

How you can help

Refer to the *Driver's Record* to see what level your learner has reached and plan their practice accordingly.

Try to think of junctions where both turns into side roads and emerges from side roads can be practised. It's a good idea to find a place where your learner can drive around a circuit or block.

When planning a location think

- will there be much traffic?
- can both turns and emerges be practised?
- are there road markings to help with positioning?
- are there any difficulties such as steep slopes or poor visibility at any of the junctions?

What to expect

The ADI will have covered the Mirror-Signal-Manoeuvre routine for dealing with junctions. Learners in the early days may be struggling with steering or changing gear while trying to think about their speed, mirrors, road position, and signs.

In addition new drivers often don't look very far ahead and

- may not see or misjudge approaching traffic
- are slow to identify potential danger

Remember, if your learner is not confident in their ability to move off they may try to emerge from a junction without stopping to see if it's safe. If you can't see that it's safe neither can they.

Don't let them cause an accident.

It's easy to see that mistakes can happen and making a mistake at a junction can be both dangerous and frightening for both of you. Keep calm and step in to help before any danger develops.

Roundabouts

Many learners find roundabouts difficult to cope with. The ADI may ask for them to be practised in stages, turning left, turning right and going ahead. If that's the case you'll need to plan routes accordingly.

Try to include a variety, from large multi-lane roundabouts to small and mini roundabouts.

How you can help

When you're approaching a roundabout tell your learner which direction you want them to go in plenty of time. If possible, use other instructions to help them such as 'sign posted to the town centre' or 'the third exit'.

Remember, at roundabouts rear end collisions are very common. They are often caused when a driver waiting to join a roundabout doesn't join when the driver behind expects them to. The driver behind then moves forward looking for traffic on the roundabout and not checking if the car in front has continued to move forward.

Be aware of this hazard at busy roundabouts.

If your learner becomes disoriented, tell them in good time where their exit is to allow them time to position correctly.

If they miss the exit don't worry. Direct them round again using the appropriate lane or road position and take the exit required. You need to encourage your learner to plan their route onto, around and off the roundabout. You should try to avoid a situation where your learner is part-way around the roundabout before they start to think about which road they should be taking.

What to expect

If your learner is uncertain of the direction they are supposed to be taking, expect incorrect signalling and positioning. They may also

- drive too slowly which can cause problems if there's fast moving traffic
- veering suddenly to take an exit at the last moment with no thought for other traffic.

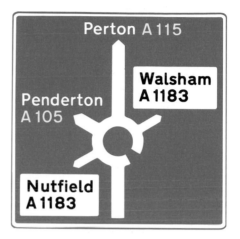

Learners often struggle with directions on roundabouts. Try to get them to make use of the signs so that they know what to expect

Pedestrian crossings

There are laws governing pedestrian crossings with which your learner must know and comply. There are also several different types of pedestrian crossing. Do you know them all?

How you can help

When your learner is approaching a crossing see if they can tell you what type of crossing it is and what rules apply.

Going out for a drive at school start and finish times should ensure plenty of opportunities to deal with busy crossings.

Darkness adds another aspect to safely dealing with pedestrian crossings, and practice in the dark is recommended.

What to expect

Noticing there's a crossing ahead is the first hurdle. You'll soon tell if your learner hasn't and you may need to act promptly. Don't let your learner over-react and stop unnecessarily. This could cause a danger to following traffic.

Remember, pedestrians are among the most vulnerable road users. If you have any doubts about your learner's ability to cope, give assistance until you're happy that they can cope unaided and without any risk of losing control.

Make certain they understand the sequence of lights at a pelican crossing and react correctly to each phase of the lights.

Dual carriageway

Dual carriageways aren't governed by the same regulations that apply on a motorway.

Driving at higher speeds and in lanes on an unrestricted dual carriageway gives valuable experience both in itself and in preparation for motorway driving once the driving test has been passed.

How you can help

As well as driving in the correct lane along the carriageway, your learner needs to gain experience of

- using slip roads
- turning right
- overtaking
- high speed traffic.

It's also valuable to let your learner experience driving on a dual carriageway in adverse weather conditions and in the dark.

What to expect

Most learners begin by driving relatively slowly. This should not be a problem when driving along the carriageway, but joining an unrestricted dual carriageway from a slip road can call for firm acceleration.

If your learner is still not confident with accelerating though the gears, wait until this skill has developed before attempting to join a dual carriageway in this manner.

Remember, vehicles ahead may want to turn right through the central reserve. Don't let your learner confuse their right signal and positioning in the right lane as a sign that they are overtaking when other clues (such as brake lights or a junction sign) show they may be turning right.

When overtaking, your learner will need to judge the length of their vehicle accurately. If they don't, there's a danger of cutting in too soon as they return to the left lane.

Turning the vehicle around

The skills needed to turn the car around in the road will be needed every time your learner has to manoeuvre in a confined space.

How you can help

You may wish to familiarise yourself with the technique your learner will have been taught by their ADI. This is explained in detail in *Driving – the essential skills*.

When looking for a place to practise the exercise consider

- the road width
- the amount of traffic you can expect
- visibility
- local residents.

Be courteous to other road users while your learner is practising. Be prepared to find somewhere else if the first place turns out to be less suitable than you first thought.

What to expect

Your learner may

- struggle with the controls
- be unable to judge the car's length
- fail to notice other road users.

Remember, a sudden loss of control when turning can result in surging forward or backwards onto the pavement and colliding with whatever is in the way. You'll need to act promptly if your learner loses control in this manner.

Some learners can take a long time to recall the techniques they've been taught. Panic can set in and they can become disoriented when half way through the exercise.

You'll need to be supportive and offer encouragement not criticism if it's all taking longer than you thought it would.

Turn to the right and then briskly to the left just before you stop

Turn to the left and then briskly to the right just before you stop

Straighten up and make sure that you stay on your side of the road

Reversing

For many learners, reversing accurately is the most difficult part of learning to drive. The statistics also show this as a key reason for learners failing the driving test.

If your learner finds reversing difficult you can expect to spend a lot of time practising this skill.

How you can help

It's easier to begin by practising reversing into a junction on the left rather than the right. The techniques for both are described in *Driving – the essential skills*.

Look for a place to practise where

- there's good visibility
- the road is level
- you don't expect much traffic
- you won't annoy local residents.

A crossroads or staggered junction is not a suitable location to practise reversing. Don't just use one location but find a variety of junctions for practice sessions

What to expect

Reversing doesn't come easily to many learners and if your learner becomes despondent then move on to another topic and return to reversing practice another day.

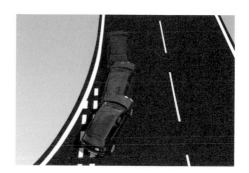

The front of the car swings out as it turns into the side road. This could endanger passing traffic

Practising on an uphill slope before skills have developed is likely to cause wear on the clutch and noise as the engine is excessively revved.

> **Remember,** good all round observation while reversing is essential.

Modern cars have an exterior mirror fitted on both sides of the car. If these mirrors are used for reversing

- there is no view directly behind the car
- the driver may focus solely on the detail seen in the mirror and fail to see other road users or obstructions
- they are not set for rear observation when driving.

Parking

On the driving test your learner may be asked to demonstrate their ability to park by reversing into a

- parking bay in a car park
- space behind another parked car on the side of the road.

> **Remember,** whether you are parking in a car park or on the side of the road your learner should be able to position the car accurately, confidently and safely.

Your ADI will have taught the procedures as explained in *Driving – the essential skills*.

How you can help

When practising reverse parking on the side of the road your learner will inevitably cause a temporary obstruction to any traffic flow. For this reason choose a quiet location for practice.

To practise reversing into a parking bay in a car park you'll need to find a car park where your learner can practise this manoeuvre.

Avoid busy car parks and peak times of day and try to find a parking bay that has an empty bay on either side. This will allow a greater margin for inaccurate steering.

While your learner's car control skills are developing you can help by being their eyes and ears, watching out for other road users. As their car control develops, you can let them become responsible for the safety aspects themselves.

As with other reverse manoeuvres, don't allow your learner to rely exclusively on the car's mirrors while reversing.

Your learner should pull up reasonably close to and parallel to with vehicle in front

Make sure your learner doesn't hit the parked vehicle and is aware of passing traffic

The car should be parked within the space of about two car lengths, close to and parallel with the kerb

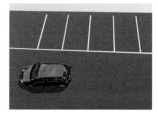

Look at the layout and the space available and decide the easiest way for your learner to park

As your learner reverses make sure they look all around for other road users

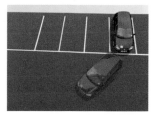

The car should be parked squarely but don't let them reverse into anything at the end of the bay

What to expect

To reverse park calls for

- accuracy
- control
- judgement.

Your learner may be weak on any or all of these skills and when your learner sets about reverse parking on the side of the road you can expect them to have trouble judging where to pull up in readiness to reverse into the space.

This may result in pulling up

- too close alongside the parked car
- too far past the parked car
- not far enough forward past the parking space.

You may find some car owners are not happy for learners to use their car to practise around and may move their vehicle.

> **Remember,** you must ensure your learner doesn't hit any other vehicle while they're practising parking.

If your learner misjudges the car's length when reversing into a parking bay in a car park, they may attempt to reverse back beyond the edge of the bay. This could result in colliding with the car park wall or barrier and damaging your car.

Emergency stop

Practising stopping the car as if there was an emergency provides valuable experience in reacting quickly and correctly while controlling the car under emergency conditions.

Practising what to do in an emergency is the only way to help your learner to cope if a real emergency situation ever arises.

> **Remember,** make certain you look around before giving any signal to stop. Relying on your additional interior mirror to tell you what's behind isn't enough.

How you can help

To practise stopping in an emergency you need to find somewhere

- with very little traffic
- where screeching tyres won't cause a nuisance
- with a good road surface.

Agree with your learner the signal to give and begin practising at low speeds. Only progress to practising at higher speeds when your learner has the control skills to cope.

What to expect

The ADI will have given instruction in the use of the controls. If your vehicle has an anti-lock braking system fitted there may be special instructions on how to achieve maximum braking. Be prepared for your learner to use excessive force when applying the brakes which may cause

- skidding accompanied by loud screeching and smoke from the tyres
- a severe jolt which could cause injury to your back or neck.

Before you give the signal to carry out an emergency stop make sure there is no following traffic. Brace yourself and prepare for a sudden rapid deceleration

Darkness

Your learner needs to practise driving in the dark since this calls for a new set of skills. As well as using the car's lights they have to learn how to cope with

- visibility when light levels are low
- glare from other vehicle's lights
- avoiding dazzling other road users.

How you can help

Unlike weather conditions, practice sessions in the dark can be planned. To give your learner as much experience as possible plan to drive on

- well lit urban roads
- unlit rural roads
- dual carriageways.

When driving in the dark, show your learner

- how to use the anti-dazzle mirror, if your car has one fitted
- how and when to dip the main beam headlights to avoid dazzling others.

When driving on rural roads without footpaths, ask them to think about pedestrians.

- Where should they be walking?
- What if they are wearing dark clothing?
- Could your learner cope?

There are rules in *The Highway Code* that give advice about parking in the dark and using the horn at night. Ask your learner if they know the rules.

What to expect

The bright lights of oncoming traffic can be difficult to cope with.

> **Remember,** in busy urban areas the glare of lights from shops and street lamps can make it easy to miss traffic lights and lights at crossings. You're responsible for making sure no mistakes are made.

If an approaching driver has forgotten to dip their headlights this can dazzle your learner and they may be unable to see the road ahead. Don't let them

- continue without reducing their speed
- retaliate by using their headlamps to dazzle the approaching driver.

Don't forget that vulnerable road users such as cyclists, pedestrians and motorcyclists may be very difficult to see in the dark.

Many people adapt to driving in the dark easily while others find it very tiring. If your learner finds it tiring be ready to end the practice session and take over the driving yourself.

Weather conditions

Adverse weather conditions such as fog, frost, high winds and rain are all common driving conditions.

In more severe weather conditions of snow and ice, be guided by the advice given out by local travel experts to determine whether the conditions are suitable for your learner.

How you can help

If the conditions aren't severe you should take the opportunity for your learner to practise as and when they arise. In bad weather your learner needs to pay particular attention to how the conditions affect their

- speed
- ability to stop
- use of windscreen wipers
- use of demisters
- need to use dipped headlights.

If the car mists up, get them to pull over and help them to demist the windows before continuing with the session.

What to expect

In today's smooth, quiet cars your learner may not realise the need for caution or how other road users are being affected. It's up to you to make sure this doesn't give rise to any risk.

Driving too close to the vehicle in front is a common mistake. Make sure the two-second rule is used and the gap increased if conditions will affect the stopping distance.

If fitted, front or rear fog lights may be used but make sure they are turned off if conditions improve.

Remember, don't think that having anti-lock brakes (ABS) will allow the car to stop regardless of the conditions. ABS will prevent the wheels from locking and so the car's steering control is not lost, but ABS cannot overcome the laws of physics; it's still possible for one or more of the tyres to skid because of

- poor road contact
- surface water
- loose road surface.

ABS does not replace the need for good driving skill.

Environmental issues

Your learner needs to understand that they can reduce exhaust emissions by driving in an environmentally friendly manner. The plus side of this is that they will save money (by using less fuel) and improve their hazard awareness skills by looking and planning further ahead.

How you can help

Your ADI should be able to explain the recommended environmentally friendly driving techniques, they can also be found in *Driving - the essential skills*. Encourage your learner to practise these techniques.

Keeping a check on the fuel consumption will show you the effect that driving in an environmentally friendly manner can have. This may encourage you to adopt these driving techniques yourself.

To help your learner appreciate environmental issues other than fuel consumption, talk about

- the importance of good maintenance, including keeping the tyres correctly inflated
- disposal of oil, old tyres and batteries.

Remember, harsh use of the accelerator and heavy braking significantly increases fuel consumption.

What to expect

Learners tend to drive more slowly than experienced drivers and this may mean they are already driving in an environmentally friendly manner.

Passengers and loads

As the driver, your learner must understand their responsibility when carrying passengers. *The Highway Code* contains the regulations that explain seat belt requirements. They must also know about the effect a load can have on a vehicle's handling and the importance of not overloading their vehicle.

It is important that your learner is made aware of their responsibilities to avoid them breaking the law.

How you can help

Letting your learner drive the car with passengers can be a valuable experience.

If any of the passengers is under 14 years of age the driver is responsible for ensuring that they are wearing a seat belt or appropriate child restraint. You should make sure that your learner is aware of this.

Use any opportunity to let your learner practise driving the car when it is loaded, such as when going on holiday.

Discuss the way extra weight can affect the vehicle and be sure to explain the importance of making sure the load is secure and not sticking out dangerously. Refer to the vehicle manufacturer's handbook for advice on altering the tyre pressures when carrying heavy loads.

What to expect

If the car is heavily loaded it's acceleration may be slower than normal. Make sure your learner takes this into account when emerging from a side road, or moving off on an uphill gradient.

If you're carrying an animal in the car, such as the family pet, it's important to keep it under control. Loose animals can be a serious distraction and could cause an accident.

If the car is filled with people there's likely to be conversations. Make sure this doesn't distract either of you

Security

Your learner needs to be aware of the importance of security. They need to be thinking about

- security of the vehicle and its contents
- their personal security.

Information about vehicle safety can be obtained from your local Crime Prevention Officer.

How you can help

When looking for a place to park the car your learner may be preoccupied thinking about the process of parking and not about the security issues.

If they choose to park in a place that has a security risk ask them if they think they have chosen a safe place to park. If necessary you should point out the risk. Make sure they understand the importance of not leaving

- the car in poorly lit areas
- valuables on display.

If your vehicle is fitted with an immobiliser and/or alarm make sure your learner is familiar with its operation and that they use it whenever they park the car.

If you have a high visibility security device, such as a steering wheel lock, show your learner how to use it.

What to expect

If your learner is naturally security conscious they will happily take measures that cut down the risks. If not, you may have to nag them to make them understand that using a car makes them a potential target for car crime; it is in their own interest to safeguard themselves and their property.

Remember, many car crimes are committed on petrol station forecourts when the driver leaves the car to pay for their fuel. Alerting your learner to the risk may prevent them from becoming a victim.

section **three**
OTHER INFORMATION

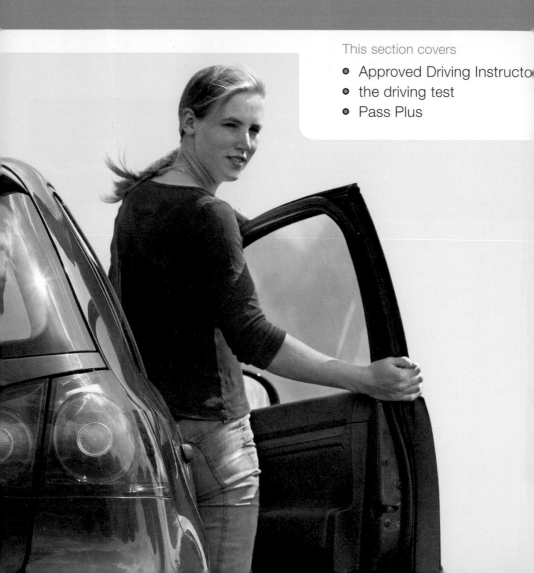

This section covers
- Approved Driving Instructo
- the driving test
- Pass Plus

Approved Driving Instructors

An ADI is approved by DSA to teach learner drivers for payment.

DSA is responsible for maintaining and checking the standards of all ADIs, who must

- have held a full driving licence for at least four years
- pass a written exam lasting 90 minutes
- pass a strict driving test
- reach and keep up a high standard of instruction. ADIs are regularly checked by a supervising examiner from DSA
- be registered with DSA
- display an ADI identification certificate on the windscreen of the tuition vehicle.

Remember, A learner must use an ADI or a trainee licence holder if they want to pay someone to teach the practical skills of driving.

Some trainee driving instructors are granted a trainee licence so that they can gain teaching experience before their qualifying examination. This licence is a pink identification certificate which must be displayed on the windscreen of the tuition vehicle.

How to choose an ADI

Your learner may ask you to help choose an ADI. You may have no experience or knowledge of local driving instructors and, rather than base your advice simply on cost, you should consider

- asking friends and relatives
- choosing an instructor who has a good reputation, is reliable and punctual and whose car suits your learner
- referring to the leaflet 'Learning to drive' which is sent out with all provisional driving licences. This explains ADI grading.

Voluntary Code of Practice

A voluntary Code of Practice has been agreed within the driving instruction industry. The code covers the following matters in relation to ADIs

- their level of qualification
- the personal conduct expected from them when giving tuition
- the professional conduct of their business
- the acceptability of their advertising
- their method of dealing with complaints.

For further information or advice contact DSA see *Useful addresses* on p3.

53

The driving test

You'll probably be anxious to know when your learner will be ready to pass their driving test.

The ADI will be able to tell you, but as a guide use these questions. If you can respond correctly to all the questions your learner should be ready to take their driving test.

The main cause of failing the driving test is inexperience. Make sure your learner is fully prepared before taking it

Can you answer yes to these questions?

Q1 Does your learner operate all the ancillary controls without any prompting?

Q2 Can your learner cope with all the situations you meet?

Q3 When you accompany your learner are you just a passenger?

Q4 Can your learner carry out all the set exercises without any assistance?

Can you answer no to these questions?

Q1 Do you ever need to reach across and use the car controls to avoid danger?

Q2 Does your learner's driving make you tense?

Q3 Does your learner hinder the flow of traffic?

Q4 Do you ever have to say to your learner 'Watch out for..'?

Pass Plus

Pass Plus is a training scheme for new drivers. Its aim is to improve their driving skills and make them safer drivers. It can also lead to insurance discounts.

The scheme has been designed by the DSA, with the help of the motor insurance and driving instruction industries, to develop their skills and knowledge in areas where they may have limited experience.

As an indicator of its effectiveness, a recent survey of L test candidates carried out by ORC International for DSA, showed that of those who had taken *Pass Plus*:

- 93% felt more confident on the road
- 89% considered that their driving skills had improved

as a result of taking the course.

Pass Plus will benefit your learner by

- enabling them to gain quality driving experience safely
- helping them to become more skillful drivers
- teaching them how to develop a positive driving style which is both enjoyable and safe
- reducing their risk of being involved in a road crash
- saving them money on their car insurance premiums.*

Pass Plus consists of a minimum of six hours' training and the emphasis is on developing practical driving skills. There is no test at the end. Instead, your learner will be assessed throughout: and they must cover all the modules to complete the training.

* Subject to status. Candidates are advised to check available discounts with participating insurance companies - a full list can be found online at www.passplus.org.uk or phone 0115 901 2633.

annex one
PRIVATE PRACTICE

When you go out driving with a friend or relative we would encourage you to record the type of driving experience that you have gained.

You can use these forms to record what you did by ticking the appropriate boxes. You'll probably tick several for each drive, for example, it may have been light when you started to drive but dark by the time you finished. Take note of the time and mileage when you start so that you can fill in how much time you spent on the road and how many miles you covered.

Fill in the time in hours (0.5h, 2.5h) and the distance in miles (20m, 47m). Don't forget to visit **www.dsa.gov.uk/drivinst/drivers-record/** for further information and to download copies of these forms.

Date	Wet roads	Dry roads	Darkness	Daylight	Dual carriageway	Country	Town and city	Overall time	Distance travelled	Comments
	◯	◯	◯	◯	◯	◯	◯	◯	◯	
	◯	◯	◯	◯	◯	◯	◯	◯	◯	
	◯	◯	◯	◯	◯	◯	◯	◯	◯	
	◯	◯	◯	◯	◯	◯	◯	◯	◯	
	◯	◯	◯	◯	◯	◯	◯	◯	◯	
	◯	◯	◯	◯	◯	◯	◯	◯	◯	
	◯	◯	◯	◯	◯	◯	◯	◯	◯	

Date																						
Wet roads																						
Dry roads																						
Darkness																						
Daylight																						
Dual carriageway																						
Country																						
Town and city																						
Overall time																						
Distance travelled																						
Comments																						

57

Date																									
Wet roads	☐	☐	☐	☐	☐	☐	☐	☐	☐	☐	☐	☐	☐	☐	☐	☐	☐	☐	☐	☐	☐	☐	☐	☐	☐
Dry roads	☐	☐	☐	☐	☐	☐	☐	☐	☐	☐	☐	☐	☐	☐	☐	☐	☐	☐	☐	☐	☐	☐	☐	☐	☐
Darkness	☐	☐	☐	☐	☐	☐	☐	☐	☐	☐	☐	☐	☐	☐	☐	☐	☐	☐	☐	☐	☐	☐	☐	☐	☐
Daylight	☐	☐	☐	☐	☐	☐	☐	☐	☐	☐	☐	☐	☐	☐	☐	☐	☐	☐	☐	☐	☐	☐	☐	☐	☐
Dual carriageway	☐	☐	☐	☐	☐	☐	☐	☐	☐	☐	☐	☐	☐	☐	☐	☐	☐	☐	☐	☐	☐	☐	☐	☐	☐
Country	☐	☐	☐	☐	☐	☐	☐	☐	☐	☐	☐	☐	☐	☐	☐	☐	☐	☐	☐	☐	☐	☐	☐	☐	☐
Town and city	☐	☐	☐	☐	☐	☐	☐	☐	☐	☐	☐	☐	☐	☐	☐	☐	☐	☐	☐	☐	☐	☐	☐	☐	☐
Overall time	☐	☐	☐	☐	☐	☐	☐	☐	☐	☐	☐	☐	☐	☐	☐	☐	☐	☐	☐	☐	☐	☐	☐	☐	☐
Distance travelled	☐	☐	☐	☐	☐	☐	☐	☐	☐	☐	☐	☐	☐	☐	☐	☐	☐	☐	☐	☐	☐	☐	☐	☐	☐
Comments																									

Date	Wet roads	Dry roads	Darkness	Daylight	Dual carriageway	Country	Town and city	**Overall time**	**Distance travelled**	Comments
	⬭	⬭	⬭	⬭	⬭	⬭	⬭	⬭	⬭	
	⬭	⬭	⬭	⬭	⬭	⬭	⬭	⬭	⬭	
	⬭	⬭	⬭	⬭	⬭	⬭	⬭	⬭	⬭	
	⬭	⬭	⬭	⬭	⬭	⬭	⬭	⬭	⬭	
	⬭	⬭	⬭	⬭	⬭	⬭	⬭	⬭	⬭	
	⬭	⬭	⬭	⬭	⬭	⬭	⬭	⬭	⬭	
	⬭	⬭	⬭	⬭	⬭	⬭	⬭	⬭	⬭	
	⬭	⬭	⬭	⬭	⬭	⬭	⬭	⬭	⬭	
	⬭	⬭	⬭	⬭	⬭	⬭	⬭	⬭	⬭	
	⬭	⬭	⬭	⬭	⬭	⬭	⬭	⬭	⬭	
	⬭	⬭	⬭	⬭	⬭	⬭	⬭	⬭	⬭	
	⬭	⬭	⬭	⬭	⬭	⬭	⬭	⬭	⬭	
	⬭	⬭	⬭	⬭	⬭	⬭	⬭	⬭	⬭	
	⬭	⬭	⬭	⬭	⬭	⬭	⬭	⬭	⬭	
	⬭	⬭	⬭	⬭	⬭	⬭	⬭	⬭	⬭	
	⬭	⬭	⬭	⬭	⬭	⬭	⬭	⬭	⬭	
	⬭	⬭	⬭	⬭	⬭	⬭	⬭	⬭	⬭	
	⬭	⬭	⬭	⬭	⬭	⬭	⬭	⬭	⬭	
	⬭	⬭	⬭	⬭	⬭	⬭	⬭	⬭	⬭	
	⬭	⬭	⬭	⬭	⬭	⬭	⬭	⬭	⬭	

Printed in the United Kingdom for The Stationery Office
173662, C200, 10/04

the **official guide to**
LEARNING
TO DRIVE

The only official guide which explains the standard required to pass the practical driving test. This book will help the learner by explaining the standard required for each key skill examined within the driving test. The aim is to make sure that the learner is capable of driving safely and confidently, without prompting from an instructor, before they take the test.

The book:

- Breaks down learning into bite sized pieces
- Explains how to structure learning with a good professional instructor and, if possible, extra practice
- Explains how to use the drivers record to ensure all key areas are covered to test standard
- Explains the standard required in each of the 24 key skills examined within the driving test

0 11 552608 0 **£7.99**

DSA®
DRIVING STANDARDS AGENCY
SAFE DRIVING FOR LIFE

5 Easy Ways to Order The DSA Range

Online
Visit www.tso.co.uk/dsa

By Telephone
Please call 0870 243 0123

By Fax
Please fax orders to 0870 243 0129

By Post
Please send orders to
Marketing, TSO,
Freepost ANG 4748,
Norwich NR3 1YX
(No stamp required)

TSO Shops
Visit your local TSO Shop

Please quote ref **CQD**